*The Christmas Light
and the Easter Hope*

To Anne Ozelle, my companion in this ministry for twenty-seven years.

THE CHRISTMAS LIGHT

and

THE EASTER HOPE

✳

Frank Johnson Pippin

Decorations by Donald Bolognese

THOMAS Y. CROWELL COMPANY

New York · Established 1834

ACKNOWLEDGMENTS

I wish to express my appreciation to the following authors and publishers for permission to quote from their copyrighted works:

G. Paul Butler for permission to quote from *Best Sermons, 1947–1948,* published by Harper & Brothers, 1948, copyright, 1947, by G. Paul Butler, and to use lines from my sermon, "The Roads We Travel," from *Best Sermons, 1949–1950,* published by Harper & Brothers, 1949, copyright, 1949, by G. Paul Butler.

Henry Holt and Company, Inc. for permission to reprint the closing stanza of "The Road Not Taken," from *Mountain Interval,* by Robert Frost; copyright, 1916, 1921, by Henry Holt and Company, Inc.; copyright, 1944, by Robert Frost.

Dodd, Mead & Company for permission to quote

the closing lines of "The House of Christmas," from *Collected Poems of G. K. Chesterton,* copyright, 1932, by Dodd, Mead & Company.

Thomas Nelson & Sons for permission to reprint passages from the Revised Standard Version of the New Testament, copyright, 1946, by the Division of Christian Education of the National Council of the Churches of Christ in the United States of America.

The Macmillan Company for permission to quote from *Behold the Man,* by Friedrich Rittelmeyer, copyright, 1929, by The Macmillan Company, and to quote from Vachel Lindsay's poem, "The Leaden Eyed," from *Collected Poems of Vachel Lindsay,* copyright, 1923, by The Macmillan Company.

Harper & Brothers for permission to quote from *What to Preach,* by Henry Sloane Coffin, copyright, 1926, by Harper & Brothers.

If I have used any quotations from other authors' works without copyright permission, I beg forgiveness.

I am deeply indebted to Miss Madge Wardell, church membership secretary, and to Miss Edna Porr, secretary to the minister, for typing and proofreading the manuscript and checking references to obtain permission to quote copyrighted material.

F. J. P.

Foreword

*

This book has been growing in my mind and spirit for several years and was finished recently during a convalescence. The first part of the book, *The Christmas Light,* consists of nine essays and two poems on the Christmas theme, which are connected only by the theme itself. Four of the offerings in this portion of the book originally appeared in other published works of mine. "The Black Shepherd," included in Part I and written last Christmas, is part fictional and part historical.

No chapters of Part II, *The Easter Hope,* have ever been published in book form before.

In the beginning it was the spirit of the great Christian holy days of Christmas and Easter that mattered most. The spirit of these days was more than a form. It was a force. In *The Christmas Light and the Easter Hope* I have tried to recapture this spirit that we might experience again the light and gladness that was Christmas, and the hope, the victory, and the joy that was Easter.

At Bethlehem the Light came "which lighteth every man that cometh into the world." In the resurrection, just beyond his cross of agony, Jesus rose above the treason of doubt and the threat of extinction to demonstrate that faith, not doubt, is final, and hope is not in vain, and that nothing is more triumphant than divine power in the arms of love. There in the dark sepulcher, sealed with a massive stone, he destroyed for all believers the chilling horror and hopelessness of "death's dateless night."

The Christmas light, therefore, shows us that every Christian can have a great present, and the Easter hope tells us that every Christian can have a great future. If this book leaves the reader with this light and hope, it will have accomplished its purpose.

F. J. P.

Leech Lake, Minnesota
July 15, 1959

Contents

✳

PART I

PART II

Part I

THE CHRISTMAS LIGHT

And the light shines in the darkness, and all
the darkness in the world has never put it out.
(Adapted from St. John 1:5)

On Keeping Christmas

✳

If one waits until Christmas Eve to start keeping Christmas, he usually finds that he has waited too long. For Christmas is not just another season or just another day. Christmas is the great fact of the centuries, around which a wealth of tradition has grown up.

Christmas is a spirit, and the spirit of Christmas is peace. Christmas is a gladness, and the gladness of Christmas is hope. Christmas is a heart, and the heart of Christmas is love. Christmas is an experience, and the experience of Christmas is giving. Christmas is a celebration, and the celebration of Christmas is Christ confessed and adored.

You see, there's a great deal to Christmas, too much to be caught on the run. And since this is true, it is suggested that all of us begin today to prepare ourselves for Christmas. Now, there is nothing unreasonable about this suggestion, because the keeping of Christmas does not depend on a full purse. It depends on a full heart.

So that our hearts may be full as the bright hour of that silver night approaches, I am inviting you to enter a covenant with your Lord to put the

Christ back into Christmas. The following sugges-
tions could help:

1. Read the world's great literature on Christmas, including the story of Christ's birth in Matthew and Luke; Dickens' *A Christmas Carol;* Van
Dyke's *The Story of the Other Wise Man;* and the
great Christmas poems, such as John Milton's "On
the Morning of Christ's Nativity"; and Chesterton's
"The House of Christmas." It is also the author's
hope that the offerings which follow in this little
book will help to generate and sustain the Christmas spirit.

2. Write letters of gratitude to those loved ones
and close friends who have meant the most to you.

3. If you are conscious of having an enemy, or
enemies, attempt a reconciliation now.

4. Schedule your shopping early so that you
will not come up to Christmas Eve with a case of
the jitters. Enter Christmas Day with your whole
self.

5. Circle your calendar now for the Christmas
services at your church and attend all of them unless
providentially hindered. Anything which generates
and interprets the Christmas spirit is of supreme
value.

6. Do something specific for someone else without any thought of recompense or return.

7. Put a love gift into Christ's stocking at Christ-

mas time. Remember, it's his birthday, and not ours that we are celebrating.

8. Resolve to give the Christ Child a new chance to grow up in your life.

9. Remember the poor, the sick, and those in prison.

10. Pray for peace.

We will never know "that first fine careless rapture" the Mother, the Magi, and the shepherds felt when first they gazed upon the face of our little Prince. But if we try, we can recapture some of the sheen and the substance of that glorious hour that moved even the angels to sing with them.

Christmas Is Coming

*

Always Christmas is coming. It is coming in December, the month of red firelight and white snow. It is coming in the calendar of the centuries, when one lone century proclaims the reality of peace on earth and good will among men. Christmas is coming in the heart that hopes.

December's Christmas is but for a day or a week at the most. The fire soon quiets into gray embers, and the snow soon melts into the earth. The gifts are soon used and old. The faces scatter into the night and are forgotten. The carol is done. Then the working world moves on, torn between progress and pain, the ideal and the real, stars and soapsuds.

The prophets hoped for better than this when they saw Christmas on the calendar of the centuries. Always Christmas was coming to the nations. At the heart of every land was Bethlehem, which means the House of Bread, with food enough to nourish all nations with good will and peace. The nations would study war no more and beat their swords into ploughshares and pruning hooks. Lands so free from greed and want and harm that each man would rest unmolested under his own vine and fig tree, and the little children would play in the streets.

And as the prophets dreamed, that Christmas is still coming.

But even more than this, Christmas is always coming in the heart that hopes. It is coming to the prodigal's father, who hears the distant but hurrying footsteps of his son hastening homeward. It is coming in the burdened soul who sees afar a cross, where he may lay down his burden of grief and guilt and his barren gain. Christmas is coming for the pilgrims of the night, haunted by a light in the window of home and marching steadfastly toward a star that marks the waiting place. It is coming to the ears of the deaf that listen intently for those lost bars of creation's imperial music. Christmas is coming to the bereaved, who see earth and heaven meet in a manger and know thereafter they are forever joined. Christmas is coming to the lonely and broken heart that believes at last in the healing of a Friend. It is coming to the troubled mind, seeking peace, the wonderful gift of God's love. Christmas is coming to the mute whose tongues are loosed with a song, left quivering above the Judean hills. It is coming to the sad of spirit as, beholding the charm of Christ, they take up the lost laughter of the universe.

The Golden Age

The Christmas story serves to point up mankind's universal and ageless longing for a golden age. For some peoples and cultures, that enchanted and happy time is a dead thing with the long and buried past. For others it is something bright and hopeful and promising, yet to come.

The ancient Greeks looked back to the golden age of Pericles and sighed that it would come no more. Later, in the Greco-Roman world, it was believed that if a man had reached the age of forty, he had seen everything that ever was and everything that ever was to be. And most everyone agreed that "life was a vain eternal recurrence, leading nowhere."

Those of the Hebrew faith and culture insisted that the golden age was yet to come. Their promised Messiah would bring their ancestral hopes, and all other good things, to pass. And in spite of the tortures of persecution and hardships that no other race has ever been called on to bear, they still scan the future for that age of peace and plenty on the earth.

The late Henry Haskell, in "Random Thoughts," his regular Sunday column in the *Kansas City Star*, said that the golden age of modern times was those halcyon years between 1890 and the outbreak of the First World War in 1914. A healing quiet had settled over the world. There was amity among the nations accompanied by a prophecy from the wise that peace had come to stay. Harvests were plentiful. World travel was virtually unrestricted. Suspicion and intrigue were apparently dead, and Europe was a paradise.

So it has ever been: some looking back at an age that is past, others looking forward to one that should come.

For us of the Christian tradition, however, the coming of the Christ Child at Bethlehem is the first and final answer. Here was the inauguration of the golden age. Poor humble shepherds were awakened to it, and they hastened from their pastures to the shrine of its joyous inception. Angels left heaven to sing about it. Aging wise men turned their backs on their old ways and their specious wisdom to mount their camels in the night and follow a star that announced the age with its silver light. The serene and holy Mother sang her haunting and lovely Magnificat while the genesis of that age still trembled in her womb. Anna and Simeon waited not in vain in the Temple, and when they saw the Child, they linked their first and final golden age forever with a Te Deum and a Nunc Dimittis: "Now lettest thou thy servant depart in peace, . . . for mine eyes have seen thy salvation, which thou hast prepared before the face of all people; a light to lighten the Gentiles, and the glory of thy people Israel."

Thus the golden age came for all peoples. And when the little Prince had grown to manhood, among the first words he uttered was that announcement, Make a new start now, for the golden age is at hand. It is not in the past. It is not in the future. It is now! Claim it for yourselves and your children! That is exactly what he said when he first came preaching: "Repent: for the kingdom of heaven is at hand." Here is heaven voicing a faith in man's possibilities. Here is the discovery of his divine self. Here is cosmic and personal backing for man's new spiritual quest, and here is a love speaking that will never let him down.

That voice still calls tonight from Bethlehem and from beyond the Jordan. Here is your golden age now, if you will have it. Old hates, suspicions, sins and fears still hush the voice. The clouds and mists of our uncertain moods still veil the star. But it is all there. It is all here, if we will have it. Our golden age. And for us there will never be another, and God will no longer countenance that cowardly prayer: "Thy Kingdom come, but not now."

"Glory to God in the highest, and on earth peace,

good will toward men." Long, dark, and unbelieving years have passed since that song was first heard above the Judean hills. But the angels are still singing it. And, if after two thousand years they are not weary of singing it, we should have the faith and courage to give the angels a rest and make that song our own.

A Baby's Tiny Cry

*

We come to Christmas again, and the journey leaves us all a year older; and, I hope, a year deeper in our understanding of life because of hardships hurdled, tasks accomplished, and victories won. We should also be a year stronger, sweeter, and more tender because of our growing sense of oneness with all elemental, living things —bluegrass sleeping under the snow; the flight of wild geese toward southern suns; the rhythm of ocean tides, and the glee of children at play; cool, shining stars, and rosebuds waiting for the spring; the goodness of wheat and the blessing of pure water; shadow and light; the ageless miracle of fire; and the good earth, patient and indestructible.

And more than anywhere else, this oneness is brought into fine focus and made articulate when we hear a baby's tiny cry. Here is something mysterious, yet certain and clear. Something that binds us and at the same time sets us free. Just one little cry, and we hear life's original and ultimate music. Just one little face, and we behold all of life—creative, purposeful, and eternal.

Here, too, is the new chance to start all over again—the past blacked out and forgotten; the present, a vital, trembling thing, and the future bright with the light of new and innocent eyes.

This happened once in a manger at Bethlehem. And ever since that night a baby's tiny cry has been the signal for rejoicing in the house; for joining hands in the innate family unity of all pure and loving hearts; and for the realization that here in this child is the greatest value and the highest good, and nothing else is really important.

Here at Bethlehem, in a baby's tiny cry, "the Word became flesh and dwelt among us, full of grace and truth . . . we have beheld his glory." And in a continuing sense, whenever a baby is born, this miracle can happen again, not only in the flesh and spirit of the cradle, but also in the lives of those who bend over it, with joy and adoration. This brings Christmas to life, and life to Christmas, and in this happy union lies our one and only hope for salvation. God became incarnate in the flesh at Bethlehem, but it is only continuing incarnations that redeem. Incarnations that prove that man is a being in whom God can dwell; and, therefore, that man's soul may be a cradle of the Eternal Love.

The Road to Bethlehem

*

There are roads and roads and roads. There is the Road of Remembrance "out to Ole Aunt Mary's," so often traveled by the Hoosier poet when he was a boy, and dreamed about a hundred times when he was old. There is the Road of True Love that runs out to Dover "through the fields of clover on our golden wedding day." There is Kipling's "Road to Mandalay, where the flyin' fishes play." There is the Road of Awakening to Damascus, the oldest living city in the world, traveled by St. Paul nineteen centuries ago. There is the Road of Fellowship to Emmaus, where the hearts of two forlorn disciples suddenly burned within them as he walked with them into the purple stretches of the twilight.

There is "The Road Not Taken," which Robert Frost remembered with a catch in his throat:

> *I shall be telling this with a sigh*
> *Somewhere ages and ages hence;*
> *Two roads diverged in a wood, and I—*
> *I took the one less traveled by,*
> *And that has made all the difference.*

But of all the roads that crawl across the earth, I love the best the Road to Bethlehem. For this is the Road of Wonder. Other things being equal, we are born on this road into a world of wonder that leaves us wide-eyed and almost breathless with the thrilling question of childhood—what next? This glad road glistens with new surprises at every turn, and a luring spray of stars is cast overhead. The greatest thing about life is living, and to live is always to keep alive the sense of wonder, romance, and expectancy. When we leave this road, we die, though our public funeral may not be held for twenty-five years.

This heaven of wonder lies about us in our infancy and in our youth. But all too soon and often our questing spirit of vision and our appetite for adventure are deadened by what we have been misled to call "the hard facts of life." Wordsworth put it this way:

The youth who daily farther from the East
Must travel, still is Nature's priest;
And is on his way attended by the Vision Splendid,
At length the man perceives it die away
And fade into the light of common day.

This was not true of the Magi from the East. Though they had grown weary and old, these wise men from the Caspian Sea still possessed the sense of wonder and awe that belongs to a little child. They left the security of their homes, turned their backs on the warmth of their firesides, bade their loved ones good-by, mounted their camels, and rode away into the night—all because of the light of a star and the wonder of a little Child. No one knows how long their journey took, nor what privations they suffered on the way, but all the world knows they finished their long trek to Bethlehem and laid their gifts of gold and frankincense and myrrh at the feet of the little Prince.

They were still chasing stars at seventy. After the long years had done their worst to them— years that leave us bowed and beaten and broken —these old men were young again when they heard the story of that wondrous Child. Their tired hearts beat a little faster, and their dim eyes were fired with a forgotten light when they saw that star. Worry, doubt, self-distrust, fear, and despair had left their telling marks upon them, but life had not got them down. These Magi from the East were still young in spirit. Their youth was still living in the ideal that keeps tempting us all to search for the Everlasting Light that shines behind all the black clouds of the world's heartbreak and woe.

The Road to Bethlehem was probably the last road they ever traveled, or at least the last long journey they ever made. But they made it, and I am sure they would tell us today that the rendezvous they kept with the lure of wonder and the call of the road was worth all it cost, for at long last that road brought them, in G. K. Chesterton's words:

To an open house in the evening . . .
To an older place than Eden,
And a taller town than Rome.
To the end of the way of the wandering star,
To the things that cannot be and are,
To the place where God was homeless,
And all men are at home.

Christmas,
Our Precious Heritage

✳

This is the season of sleigh bells and snow. The myriad lights of Yuletide break up the night and make it beautiful. The silver chimes ring out the time. The people, light of heart and eager-faced, throng the merry streets. The shops within resound with the happy humming of clerks and customers and the cash-sale clang of the busy registers. With the slightest tinkle of their tiny bells the lads and lassies of the Salvation Army call from the passing parade for us to remember the poor.

Half-grown forests of spruce, balsam, cedar, and fir trees, having lost their earthly moorings somewhere, stand now in little, rootless regiments along the boulevards, a little lonely and waiting to be bought for a pretty price and taken into custody. There is a spicy tang in the crisp, cold air. Children romp home from school a little early and blow their warm breath against the cold to see it turn to cloudlets of frost and fog. The sweet melody of "Silent Night, Holy Night" drifts our way from a narrow valley beyond, and from over the hill floats the quaint old tune, "The First Noel."

Mother is stirring up cakes and cookies for the oven and cleaning house and remembering back and looking forward. Father is out somewhere trying to catch up with his portion of the world's work. He remembers, too, and looks forward. The postman, in a hurry and out of breath, is making double rounds with sheaves of cards and letters, and packages done in designs of holly, mistletoe, and bright red berries. All are the outward symbols and signs of our deep, inward heritage—Christmas.

This rich heritage of ours started with a Mother and a Child and a radiance shed upon old manger wood. It was further enhanced with angels singing among the stars, wise men following a Light with gifts of gold and frankincense and myrrh, and shepherds breaking the tedium of their long night watches to hasten to a little crib and there behold the glory of God shining in the face of a newborn Prince.

Ever since that night, when Mary came to a stable door, Christmas has been a time of enchantment. It is a time when every man becomes a boy again and, as Emerson said, the huge globe becomes a toy. Christmas is a time of bright-eyed wonder. Long ago my brothers and I used to mount the hills of home on Christmas Eve and search the jeweled sky for the Star in the East. We swept the eastern heavens with eye and hand and will until we could point with pride to that star that outshone all the twinkling starry host clustered around it. Then we ran home to announce our amazing discovery, only to be laughed at by our elders, who of course knew better.

But did they? Sometimes I think we were wiser than they. Sometimes I think we found that star. This is the enchantment and wonder of Christmas. This is the sixth sense that tells us, who are growing old together, that the simple faith that filled our boyish eyes actually saw that star, that it was up there blazing in splendor just for us. This is the wonder made of wisdom that tells us, beyond the rim of youth, that the children are always right.

But the heritage of Christmas sings and speaks to us of even deeper things. It sings of peace, the wonderful gift of God's love, the peace that keeps all men serene, who bear good will to their fellows. It speaks to us of majesty and strength, and the Prince of Peace, whose Kingdom will outlast all the kingdoms of the world. "His name shall be called Wonderful . . . The Prince of Peace. Of the increase of his government and peace there shall be no end." Christmas speaks to us of an abiding presence: "And they shall call his name Emmanuel, which being interpreted is, God with us." It announces redemption in the transforming

20

power of a name: "Thou shalt call his name Jesus: for he shall save his people from their sins."

Christmas tells us that this is the time to give and forgive; this is the season for charity and mercy, when the noblest emotions of the human spirit express themselves without caution or fear of cost. Christmas presents itself as the ageless custodian of all beautiful and tender things—like snow that lies upon the winter hills, like love that melts our hearts of stone, and like flowers that still bloom in the half-forgotten woodlands of our childhood.

Christmas buries the old and brings the new to pass. Once each twelve months Christmas tiptoes on silken, silent feet up to the old, dying year and with magic hands tucks it away into bed with a song that makes all the years to come forever new. Christmas lights the fire over the hearth, spreads the feast beyond the cheery flames, places the welcome mat outside the open door, and then calls home again the last, the least, and the lost.

How High Is Your Star?

∗

"The star . . . came and stood over where the young child was . . ." (St. Matthew 2:9)

When we coast on snow from the hills to the river, we discover a profound and exciting law of life: "The higher we start, the farther we go." In other words, the altitude from which we start determines the distance we shall travel.

As we look back over our lives in this Christmastide, most of us know in our hearts that we have not gotten as far in life as once we dreamed that we would go. One probable reason for this is that there was something lacking in the altitude from which we started. The star we chose to guide us was not high enough. You see, it is altitude that gives us distance. In view of this law of life, let me ask: How high is your star?

Ralph Waldo Emerson said: "Hitch your wagon to a star." This is all very well, but the Sage of Concord didn't say which star. And that is the important point. There are so many stars, and few are high enough to give us the distance we need for our long journey.

There is the Star of Convenience by which the innkeeper was guided the night Mary came to a stable door. The owner of that little hotel in the City of David refused to take the sacrament of the inconvenient and thus robbed himself of the one grand opportunity of his humdrum life—that of playing host for the first time to the Son of God and of being the first, besides Joseph and Mary, to see the newborn Prince. The Star of Convenience never sheds a pretty light and always robs us of greatness. It is not high enough to give us much distance, and yet how many of us today are guided by what is, or what is not, convenient! How high is your star?

There is the Star of Expediency which guided Herod and Pilate. What will people say? comprised the chief motivation of their confused lives, and they stood against anything that threatened their political and social position—right or wrong. So while Herod the Great failed in his bloody plot to murder Jesus as a child, Pilate and another Herod got him at the cross. Their little lives were guided solely by the Star of Expediency, and most often that star throws a ghastly light. It is a low star, too. It is much too low to give us the distance we deeply need for our perilous journey. And yet how many millions are guided entirely by what is, or what is not, expedient! How high is your star?

There is the Star of Personal Gain which guided the Sadducees. They believed not in Christ, nor the resurrection. They possessed certain commercial rights and privileges and they played their tricky cards for all they were worth. They had the trading and money-exchange concessions at the Temple, made a racket of religion, and waxed rich and fat from the Temple routine and feast days. On one occasion at least, Jesus drove them, or their underlings, from the Temple Court, accusing them, between whiplashes, of making God's house of prayer a den of thieves. And then these money merchants of their time vowed that Christ must die.

The Star of Gain which guided them cast only a partial and unsteady light. The Sadducees never discovered that mere things cannot satisfy the deep hungers and thirsts of the soul. They never found the treasures that money cannot buy. Their star was too low to give them any altitude, any perspective. Not high enough for men made in the image of God. So they lived and died in the shallows, and that tide in the affairs of the Kingdom that leads us on to the fortunes of God never bore them out into the depths of the life beautiful. How high is your star?

There is the Star of Bethlehem which guided the wise men from the Caspian Sea—Caspar, Melchior, and Balthazar. This star came and stood over the place where the young Child was. This is the Star of Home because it is the Star of Jesus. At long last these scholars of the stars found that this Star of Bethlehem was the highest and most wondrous and meaningful star of all. Doubtless in their youth and middle years, these Magi from the East had followed many other stars that left them disillusioned. They burned into ash and cinders and left them in the dark. Only when they had grown old did they find and follow the highest star, the right star.

They had all but waited too long to come where their real heart had always wanted to be. Yet they finally made life's gladdest discovery: No star that leaves us anywhere short of Bethlehem is high enough for anyone made in the spiritual image of God. Only when we come and stand over the place where the Christ Child is do we travel with delight and ultimate arrival. This unique star sheds a pretty light, as constant as the North Star in the heavens on a winter's night. This is the only star with enough altitude for the journey we pilgrims must go.

The Star of Bethlehem that haunted the singing angels out of heaven puts real distance into our lives. It guides us to the farthest outreaches of the meaning and power of prayer. It sheds an unvarying light into our study and meditation of the living Word of God, "the Word was made flesh, and dwelt among us." This light escorts us into the harvest fields of Christian service. It awakens us to a genuine concern for humanity, that we may dwell in genuine brotherhood and peace. And best of all, this star leads us gently to the home of the spirit, as it did the Magi long ago.

The Black Shepherd

*

Some of the shepherds called him Simon the Mute, and others referred to him as the Black Shepherd. But he was not totally mute. He was partially deaf, and could stammer a few broken words. He had a limp in his right leg, but he was exceptionally strong and tall, with shocks of raven black hair and piercing black eyes. Another thing that set him apart from the other shepherds was the shining ebony of his unblemished skin, several shades darker than their dark brown. And because of the strange law of compensation, he could see better than all the other shepherds put together.

Simon appeared out of the nowhere one spring day when he was only a lad. He joined the old men in Shepherds Field just outside of Bethlehem. Agreeing to his becoming a shepherd's boy for only his keep, the wizened, bearded, old men took him on.

As the years passed, Simon learned much from the aging shepherds. He learned where the greenest and richest grasses grew, the difference between nourishing and poisonous herbs and grasses, and he learned to instill confidence and contentment in the sheep he led and fed. He learned all the sheep by name and the shepherds' call that took them straightway into tow when they showed signs of wanderlust. He also learned to be thorough and gentle in the shearing.

However, the older shepherds could never get very much out of Simon. When their curiosity could stand it no longer, they would bellow out at him in a cross fire of questions, but his deafness and his stuttering tongue usually left them in confusion.

"Where do you come from?" they would shout.

"Era-ne-E-ra-ne," he seemed to say.

"There is no such place in all of Judea or Galilee!" Then Simon would stammer in a strained whisper, "Era-ne-E-ra-ne," and suddenly become quiet. Whenever they asked him about his house and lineage, the name of his father and mother, he would groan deeply, let out a shrill cry, then fall face down in the grass, weeping bitterly. They soon despaired of learning anything about his past and so let him alone. Nevertheless, as Simon grew from boyhood into youth, the older shepherds began to have a hidden respect for him, although they shunned him most of the time. He was the first to sense danger and the last to give up the search after the sheep. He never fell asleep in the night watches. He lay on his back at times and counted the stars, naming them after the sheep he had grown to love. Then he would take long walks around his sleeping charges, alternately trying to chant and hum a tune that sounded, even in its fragments, the long sadness and loneliness of the world.

On one of these nights when the others were in the dead of sleep, the Black Shepherd lay with his face toward the eastern heavens, counting the stars again and naming them after the sheep. On this signal night there were banks upon banks of stars, and his shining black eyes kept piercing through them, searching for those that were hard to find. Suddenly something like a giant topaz swam out of infinity into view, and hovered over Bethlehem as the brightest and most dazzling jewel of heaven. Simon jumped to his feet to awaken his fellow shepherds, and suddenly he heard faintly a song from the skies. He stood still, gazing upward. He strained his feeble ears to hear, and then he saw a multitude of angels. He limped toward the sleeping shepherds, dragging his right leg, but they were already awake and on their feet. They stood at first frozen in their tracks, and then they started dancing around in a circle, clapping their hands with joy and shouting ever louder and louder, "Hallelujah! Hallelujah!"

The Black Shepherd stood outside of the circle groaning deeply within and trying in vain to ask them what was this marvelous thing that had come to pass. But before he could frame any intelligent words, the other shepherds broke the circle and bolted away toward Bethlehem, never once turning around to see what had happened to the Black Shepherd, who was limping at a long distance behind them.

When the Black Shepherd finally arrived at the stable, he found the other shepherds crowded within, and behind them the press of a great crowd. He could not break through and so he sat down, a few yards away, on the steps of the old inn and cried. Then he slipped away into the night and was never seen again in Shepherds Field outside of Bethlehem.

After his disappearance, the old shepherds, who hired him when he was a boy, wondered and talked about him in their long night watches. They missed him deeply and they were always sorry that they had shunned him. Especially did they regret that, in their haste and thoughtlessness, they had robbed him of the chance to answer the invitation of the angels to go and see where the Christ Child lay.

They never knew that the Black Shepherd returned to the ancient North African city of Cyrenaica, where he was born. When home, he remembered the lofty hill on which his city was built 631 years before. And on its summits he would lie on balmy spring days and look out ten miles to the sea. His native city was once the center of Greek learning and culture, but it began to decay when the Romans took it over several years before his birth. Disillusioned upon his return to his native haunts, the Black Shepherd became a wanderer, traveling as far as the Bahr Lut, then skirting this dead sea of salt over into Moab and Perea. He also journeyed into Phoenicia and down the coast to Joppa, where the vivid blue Mediterranean was a balm to his lonely and hungry heart.

After more than thirty years of aimless wanderings, earning his bread in whatever way he could, a strange, inexplicable intuition urged the Black Shepherd to go to Jerusalem. He arrived during the Jewish Passover and found the Holy City in turmoil. The religious authorities were trying a young man from Nazareth for blasphemy, and the civil authorities were trying him as an enemy of the state. Inquiring of everyone he encountered, the Black Shepherd found that his name was Jesus, that he was born many years ago in Bethlehem. He also learned that the Nazarene had been condemned to die a felon's death on a cross. It was a dark Thursday night, and the Black Shepherd could not sleep.

Early on Friday morning he saw a crucifixion processional forming for the Place of the Skull, which was just outside the city on a hill called Calvary. Halfway up the hill he found an opening in the mob, and he edged his way through them to the first row that lined the cruel passage upwards. Glancing to his right, he beheld the young man bearing his cross and approaching with slow and wobbly steps. As he drew up to the Black Shepherd, he winced and fell beneath his cross. The crowd roared with threats and jeers. Then there was a sudden stillness in the mob.

In the brief quiet, Jesus turned and looked at the Black Shepherd as he had never been looked at before. The black eyes of the condemned man looked deep into the Black Shepherd, and there was a pleading in his ageless eyes for help—a pleading the Black Shepherd could not resist. Though stooped and weakened by the many long years, the Black Shepherd lifted the scourged and condemned Jesus from the dirty stones, wiped the grime and blood from his face, then shouldered his cross for him. With the Nazarene by his side, the Black Shepherd started the processional again, urged on by the cracking whips and shouts of the soldiers. The cross pressed heavily upon his back. The condemned one spoke: "You are Simon of Cyrene." Then a miracle happened, and the Black Shepherd's ears were opened, and his tongue was loosed in the very naming of his name by one who knows the names of us all.

"Yes, I am," the Black Shepherd answered. "I was a youth keeping watch over the flock in Shep-

herds Field the night you were born in Bethlehem.
But you see, I have a limp, and the other shepherds
raced ahead of me to the manger, and when I arrived I could not get near you because of them and
the press of the crowd from the town."

"Simon, you have no limp. And now my cross
is light upon your back." And so it was. A strange
music filled the Black Shepherd's heart, and a new
strength that straightened his back so that he pressed
up toward Golgotha under the cross, bearing his
burden with a stout heart. As they approached the
top of the knoll, the Black Shepherd was discon-
solate again at the thought of the cruel and igno-
minious crucifixion of his new friend. "What can I
do? What can I do?" he cried.

"Fear not, Simon," the Master answered, "the
suffering will not be long . . . and then the glory
. . . I will rise from death never to die again."

The Black Shepherd watched there with John
and Mary, the Blessed Mother, and with the other
tearful women at the cross. He heard the words that
fell from the parched lips of the Crucified. And
imprinted indelibly in his memory was the answer
Jesus gave to a thief who was dying with him:
"Lord, remember me when you come into your
kingdom."

"Today thou shalt be with me in paradise."

When the vile deed was done, the Black Shepherd followed Joseph of Arimathea, with the body, to Joseph's new tomb. Then he saw Joseph and his attendants quietly lay the body away and cap the fragrant tomb with a large, thick slab of stone.

The Black Shepherd found it hard to explain his emotions. For some unearthly reason he was not sad. He was alive as he had never been alive before. He somehow knew the tomb could not be the end, and all his inconsolable grief was forever gone. He thought with a new mind and felt with a new heart. The surging of a new strength within him thrilled him with a nameless ecstasy.

The Black Shepherd hurried away from Joseph's garden and headed for Cyrene, the capital city of Cyrenaica. As he hastened along the rugged way, fragments of Jesus' words came back to him: "And then the glory!" He shouted them against the mountains and declaimed them with sweeping gestures to the skies.

After many days the Black Shepherd approached his native city standing on the lofty hill. He stopped and gazed upward at its new beauty and feasted on the meadows and valleys around him below the city. In a sudden flashback of the years, the Shepherds Field, Bethlehem, the star, and the angels' song flooded his memory like a clean, sweet tide. He heard the sky-born melody again and all the words, denied him on that Holy Night when Christ was born:

"Fear not, for, behold, I bring you good tidings of great joy, which shall be to all people. For unto you is born this day in the city of David a Saviour, which is Christ the Lord."

"Glory to God in the highest, and on earth peace, good will toward men!"

The Black Shepherd shouted them up toward his towering city, and by the time he reached its streets he had gathered them into the melody he heard as a youth above the Judean hills.

There were not many earthly years left to the Black Shepherd in the beautiful province of Cyrenaica, but he spent them all telling everyone he met that it is never too late. And whenever they would listen, he would prove these glad tidings with his own happy story and with the melody and words of the angels' song.

Christmas Has Come!

✳

Christmas is God's declaration of war against little-ness. The enfeebling littleness in the three tenses that grip our lives. It is little and ruinous, for instance, to nurse a gnawing remorse over a shabby and sordid past, because that event in Judea made forgiveness personal and possible to all peoples. While nothing is more familiar to us than an old mistake, it is also true that nothing is more futile than regret. Why regret? Christmas has come! And the spirit of Christmas has a magic way of healing old wounds and covering old scars. By our leave, Christmas has a way of putting the past to bed.

It is also little and damaging to worry unduly over the present. There is no therapy in worry. There are only thongs. That splendid act of extrav-agance beyond the stable door made this hour good. So why worry? Christmas has come! This means Emmanuel, God is with us, which is another way of saying that his warm spirit of boundless love is with us. And that spirit has a way of charg-ing present moments with the enchantment and delight of meaningful friendships, fruitful giving and receiving, and fireside and home.

Another habit that whittles us down is anxiety

over the future. But why be anxious? Christmas has come! And with it the bright spirit of hope that cushions us against the shocks that tomorrow may bring. Yes, there was a cross beyond the manger, but there were also lilies in bloom beyond the cross. Easter lilies. And from a timeless and unconquerable spirit there was a shout: "The Lord God omnipotent reigneth!"

This greening spirit fills our souls with a keen expectancy because something wonderful is always about to happen. Such a spirit possessed the shepherds and the Magi, and it had long overflowed in the pure heart of the Blessed Mother. And something wonderful did happen! What is more, it will keep happening down through all the coming years to us who trust that God will walk with us through our tomorrows as he did our yesterdays. Even in this disquieting hour we believe this. We believe it because the Christ Child grew up into something big enough to cover the three tenses of our lives— the past, the present, and the future.

As at Bethlehem under a star, so today wherever we are, the little Lord Jesus brings us a mood, a music, and a message that never shall cease their strange stirrings of life and wonder in our hearts.

The Nativity

*

Beneath a blazing star in Bethlehem,
In the crisp stillness of a far gone night,
Within a stable reeking, dark, forlorn,
Pierced sparsely by the silver shafts of light,
Jesus Christ, the Son of God, was born . . .

To silhouette the profile of God's face
Against the darkness of our tragedies;
To stamp his truth on ev'ry fallen race,
And heal the wounds of our adversities.

The glow of love within the Virgin's heart
Pulsing loud against fresh-scented hay;
A sweet, clear angels' song heard far away—
All looked upon the Child and called him good.

This giant topaz turned the stable cells
Into a shrine for such virginity
That lured the shepherds from their ancient hills
And the wise men from the Caspian Sea.

Peace! Peace on earth! in this new Christmastide,
As God with men and men with God abide.
Eternal Star, with all thy power of gem,
Shine on, make ev'ry town a Bethlehem!

Christmas Seal

*

I broke the Seal of Christmas through,
And found the things I wish for you:

The white peace of the snow that lies
On winter hills against the skies.

The song the angels sang that night
To put the world's dark fears to flight.

The joy the startled shepherds had
To thrill their hearts and make them glad.

The love the blessed Virgin bore
To her small Son upon the floor.

The glow of that Star's silver fire
To purge you from all gross desire.

And absolution from all sin,
The presence of the Lord within.

Part II

THE EASTER HOPE

*

*"If in this life only we have hope in Christ,
we are of all men most miserable."*
    (From St. Paul in First Corinthians 15:19)

"Because I live, ye shall live also."
        (From Jesus in St. John 14:19)

Easter as a Church Festival

*

Long before the Christian era, the rugged Teutons
and the Angles and Saxons paid honor to Eastre,
their famed goddess of light and spring. It was
their Easter—a popular festival held in April to
celebrate the death of winter and the birth of
spring. To these ancient harbingers of modern civ-
ilization, the coming of spring was something tremendous. Isolated from the adventures of life by
the cold, rigorous winter, their armies could now
march again, and their ships reset their sails for
the barter of grain and gold. The poetic name of
their goddess suggests east, dawn, and spring. In
this festival to Eastre were included many customs
and practices, supposedly gathered from the widely
varied pre-Christian mythologies. One was the ex-
change of eggs, considered as a symbol of rebirth
and resurrection. Another was the burning of fires
to celebrate the triumph of spring over winter.

Now, according to witnesses, one Jesus arose
from the dead in Jerusalem in the fourth decade of
the first century, and for seven centuries his followers celebrated this event without a popular name
for its deep significance. While it is true that the
word "Easter" appears in the old authorized ver-

sions of the New Testament, it is found only in one passage—Acts 12:4. This is a mistranslation, however, as the original is "Pascha," the ordinary Greek word for Passover—a feast in memory of Israel's freedom from the tyranny of the Pharaohs. All of the newer versions of the New Testament properly employ the word "Passover."

It was not until the eighth century that the name Easter was taken over from this pagan festival by the Anglo-Saxons and transferred to the Christian festival, designed to celebrate the resurrection of Jesus Christ. Hardly any of its primitive, colorful significance was lost in the transfer. The feast was rather enhanced with a historical fact that, like the spring, has given hope and meaning to human existence. Hearkening back to a custom of pre-Christian days, little children still hunt their hidden eggs on Easter, but they are now colored with a new significance by virtue of their attachment to the most inspiring event of world history.

In the early centuries Easter was set apart among Christians for baptism, and the Latin name for the following Sunday, *Dominica in albis*—Sunday in white—preserves for us the memory of the custom of those new converts wearing their white robes throughout the week. Those in the new faith greeted each other with the kiss of peace and the salutation, "Christ is risen!" to which the glad response was, "He is risen, indeed!" (This custom is still observed in many Eastern Orthodox groups.) In medieval times, in some of the French cathedrals, a sacred game of ball was played by the bishops, canons, and other leaders of the church, and as late as the fifteenth century rhythmical dances were executed to the strains of weird music. To these were added shows in which even the clergy joined, reciting stories and legends from the pulpit to stir up laughter among the hearers.

For three centuries the proper time for the observance of Easter was a subject of controversy between the eastern churches giving allegiance to Byzantium and the western churches with their center in Rome. The cleavage also lay between Christians of strictly Judaistic background and Christians of non-Jewish or Gentile heritage. The eastern group set the date on the fourteenth day of the first Jewish month, Nisan, to coincide with the Jewish Passover. The western group insisted that the celebration be held the first Sunday after the fourteenth, that it might stand alone to commemorate the resurrection of Jesus. The matter was finally settled at the Council of Nicaea, called by Constantine the Great in Asia Minor in 325 A.D. Of deep historical interest also is the fact that this same council denounced the well-known Arian heresy then threatening the foundations of Christendom and formulated in stern opposition to it the Nicene Creed, the first creed Christendom ever had. Divisions among the churches were threatening the solidarity of Constantine's empire, and to encourage attendance upon this important and first ecumenical council, the emperor paid the transportation of all the delegates out of the Roman treasury.

The decision at Nicaea makes Easter a movable feast, so that it falls upon the first Sunday after the full moon which happens upon or next after March 21. If the full moon happens upon a Sunday, Easter day falls upon the succeeding Sunday. The object of this arrangement was to prevent Easter from falling on the same day as the Jewish Passover. With the exception of a few Communions, who have through the years refused to abide by the Nicaean decision, this method of determining the date for Easter is generally accepted today. The Christian festival, therefore, is never before March 22 and never after April 25. The latest Easter in this century occurred in 1943 on April 25. Only twice in the last two centuries has it fallen on March 22.

It is interesting to note that Easter has inspired the observance of a series of special days and seasons, characterized on the one hand by deep solemnity and on the other by great joy. While most Protestants and other non-Catholic groups do not strictly and sacerdotally observe all these days and seasons, as we find them observed in the three Catholic traditions (Roman, Anglican, and Eastern Orthodox), they should be mentioned in order to indicate the great emphasis the early Church placed upon the resurrection. Furthermore, these special days and seasons are encouragements to the Christian's devotional life and the necessity of sacrifice and penitence, and as such they are, of course, significant for Christians of all Communions.

There is Lent, called a fast, a period of forty days preceding Easter, not including Sundays, devoted to self-denial and penitence. The early Church took this idea from the forty days of temptation and fasting our Lord faced and endured in the wilderness prior to his embarking upon his public ministry. The first day of Lent is Ash Wednesday, so named from an ancient custom of strewing ashes over the head as a sign of penitence. Today the priest makes an ash cross on the forehead of the penitent. The day preceding Ash Wednesday is Shrove Tuesday, a final day of merriment, feasting, and fun, as still observed in the Mardi Gras. There is Palm Sunday, one week before Easter, which commemorates the triumphal entry of Jesus into Jerusalem. The following Monday opens Passion Week, or Holy Week, which deals with the events of our Lord's last week in and around Jerusalem, including his crucifixion and burial. In this week there are Maundy Thursday, commemorating the institution of the Lord's Supper with his disciples; Good Friday, the day he was crucified; and Holy Saturday, on which in the Catholic church the first Easter Mass is held, and which closes the period of Lent.

Easter as the Historical Basis
of the Christian Faith

*

On Good Friday right was on the scaffold and
wrong was on the throne. On Easter morning they
changed places. Wrong was nailed to the scaffold,
and right broke the shackles of death and mounted
up to claim her rightful throne. According to un-
relenting testimony, Jesus of Nazareth had risen
from the dead. The scoffing crowd challenged him
to come down from the cross. He did what was
better. He accepted the suffering and came from the
tomb. Those first disciples were quickened out of
despair by this startling event, and the resurrection
at once became the historical basis of the new faith.
As they viewed it, the death of Jesus was a brutal
tragedy, and if Calvary had been the last chapter
in the life of one who claimed to be the Son of
God, if this miracle of mastery and manhood had
met ultimate defeat at the hands of evil forces, then
the whole scheme of righteousness would have re-
ceived a death blow, and the premise of the Caesars
would have remained forever inviolate. Disillusioned and despairing, the disciples could not have
carried on. His resurrection revealed that Jesus'

ideal for a new world order was backed by the universe.

Their religious emotions were grounded now in an incontestable fact, and with this consciousness a new passion was born to present the claims of their Friend and Conqueror upon the heart of the race. At last their minds were clear about the involved questions of duty and destiny and the innate worth of all human life. Easter morning had done this. It assured these disciples that God was not only behind the scenes, but also in the scenes.

Thus the daring testimony to the resurrection of Jesus constitutes the historical basis of the Christian faith. "If Christ be not raised, your faith is vain; ye are yet in your sins" (I Cor. 15:17). Without that open tomb and the glorified one who came forth from it, there would have been no Pentecost, and, therefore, no Church. Those who have denied the resurrection have made little contribution to genuine scholarship and done very little to deepen the spiritual life of the people. They hasten to draw encouraging analogies from the resurrection and apply them to daily living in terms of a conquering, risen life. They thus make the resurrection merely a pretty parable of life, when as a matter of fact the resurrection was God's great enduring act of history for all time. What happened in Joseph's guarded garden also became God's

Word to all who dare to believe that Jesus wiped the grave dust from his eyes and came forth from the darkness of the sepulcher to hold forth a victory over life and sin and death for every believing personal soul.

I attended the formation of the World Council of Churches in Amsterdam as a reporter in 1948, and in my fading notes on God's Word for our world I find this paragraph:

"There is a Word of God for our world. It is that the world is in the hands of the living God, whose will for it is wholly good; that in Christ Jesus, his incarnate Word, *who lived and died and rose from the dead,* God has broken the power of evil once for all and opened for everyone the gate into freedom and joy in the Holy Spirit; that the final judgment on all human history and on every human deed is the judgment of the merciful Christ; and that the end of history will be the triumph of his Kingdom, where alone we shall understand how much God has loved the world."

This historic assembly of Christian theologians and leaders from practically every nation under heaven realized, in facing the question of the resurrection, that those who deny it as a historical event ignore in their denial the common axiom of all learning and truth: that reality is larger than any individual or group intelligence.

This axiom must be accepted before one can approach the tremendous fact of the resurrection of Jesus as a sheer miracle of the Eternal's power. Unless a man breaks down and admits that he knows everything, he cannot well deny the most bold and revolutionizing event of world history. Furthermore, there are many today who do not believe in this fact of hope, because they have not been introduced, or rather have not introduced themselves, to the realm of spiritual realities of which our Lord's resurrection is an integral part. What with the Sadducees, the Pilates, and the Herods, this was true in the first century of Christian history.

But, happily, there remain those today who have built an altar around this strong, beautiful fact, and, as in the first days, they have become happy hosts who had rather sing through this Easter symphony of triumph than argue about it. They feel it to be true when they have looked into their hearts, and know it when they have reviewed the indelible facts.

A brief review of these facts, and what they portend for the life of the Christian in the twentieth century, is at once necessary and timely. Cardinal among these, let us repeat, is that what the disciples of Christ said happened on Easter morning constitutes the historical basis of the Christian faith. If we do not discover the basis of the Christian faith and life in the historical facts of the resurrection of Jesus, we need not look elsewhere. This faith then has no basis and can readily be relegated to the scrap heap of the cults. If we learn of the life and self-inflicted martyrdom of Socrates from the Dialogues of Plato, we learn of the life, death, and resurrection of Jesus from sources that are equally, if not more, reliable. And who doubts the life and death of Socrates?

While this body of testimony is somewhat lengthy and involved, certain clear facts stand out beyond the prospect of dislodgment. First, there is Jesus' own prediction as to what would happen on the third day after Calvary. Time and again this prophecy is on his lips. With it he confounded the disbelieving Sadducees: "Ye do err, not knowing the scriptures, nor the power of God." He cited the experience of Jonah for an analogy of his own: that "as Jonah was three days and three nights in the belly of the whale, so will the Son of man be three days and three nights in the heart of the earth."

He faced his foes who would do him to death to tell them that if they destroyed the temple (speaking of his body) "in three days I will raise it up." He repeatedly foretold his resurrection to his disciples, linking with it all the attending circumstances of his march to Jerusalem, the humiliation his enemies bore him, the betrayal of Judas Iscariot, and his ultimate demise upon the cross. In fact, he seldom spoke of his sufferings without speaking in the same breath of his resurrection. And before the shadows of Golgotha closed in upon him, he identified himself with the resurrection as he prepared to call Lazarus from the grave. The words were spoken to Mary and Martha, the sorrowing sisters of their dead brother: "I [myself] am the resurrection, and the life: he that believeth in me, though he were dead, yet shall he live: and whosoever liveth and believeth in me shall never die." Then upon his call, Lazarus came forth from the grave alive, vindicating the prophecy and power of the Son of God not only about himself, but every living child of the heavenly Father.

Secondly, a large body of accumulative testimony converges upon the central conclusion that Jesus arose from the dead, as he predicted, leaving an empty tomb behind him, and made some twelve appearances to prove it. The earliest account we have of his victory over death is I Corinthians 15, written by St. Paul about 56 A.D., within the living memory of the generation to which Jesus belonged. As to the authenticity of this manuscript, even Renan, the French skeptic, admitted "that the Corinthian correspondence came from the pen of St. Paul is undisputed and undisputable." This priceless document sets forth four essential convictions held in common by all true Christians of that day. (1) That Christ died for our sins and was buried. (2) On the third day he arose again. (3) He appeared to certain persons. (4) He ascended and remains in a state of exaltation. "He was buried, and he rose again the third day." We see that his rising on the third day is connected definitely with his burial so as to give his resurrection a place among datable and weighable events.

This Pauline account of the Easter event points out six postresurrection appearances, and to one of them there were more than five hundred witnesses. The four Gospels, which were written later, make mention of six more appearances, excluding their repetition of some of those mentioned in this Corinthian document. Taken together, these five sources record that approximately six hundred interested followers of the New Way were eyewitnesses of their resurrected Lord. Included among his appearances were those to Mary Magdalene, Mary the mother of James, Joanna and "the other women"; to Simon Peter, to the ten disciples without Thomas; to the eleven with Thomas; to Cleopas and another disciple on the Emmaus road; to James; to the seven by the sea of Galilee; to more than five hundred brethren at once; to all the apostles, probably including the seventy, and to the disciples at the Ascension. As for the disciples themselves, they were so impressed and overjoyed with what they had seen in the person of their risen Leader and Lord, they immediately concluded that their chief function was to be a "witness of the resurrection." (Acts 4:33) They went so far as to make this eyewitness experience an indispensable qualification for apostleship itself, as for example, when they chose Matthias to take the place of Judas (Acts 1:23) and when St. Paul referred to his eyewitness experience to support his claim to authentic apostleship. (I Cor. 1:9)

Our third consideration is the reliability and credibility of this body of testimony against which there have been many unsuccessful attacks. The most common and general among these is the contention that Jesus arose spiritually but not bodily. Jesus answered this himself. Speaking to the disciples who were questioning whether this were the case, supposing "that they saw a spirit," he said: "Why do questionings rise in your hearts? See my hands and my feet, that it is I myself; handle me and see; for a spirit has not flesh and bones as you see that I have." Then he showed them his hands and his feet, and while they still questioned and wondered, he said: "Have you anything here to eat?" They then gave him a piece of broiled fish, and he ate it before them. (Luke 24:36–43) They never doubted thereafter. It may also be said in this connection that unless we speak of a bodily resurrection, we need not speak of any resurrection at all, for it was only his body that was buried. At the last hour upon the cross he committed his spirit into his Father's keeping with the memorable words: "Father, into thy hands I commend my spirit."

It has also been said that the credibility of the witnesses cannot be taken seriously. Quite the contrary is true, because they had every opportunity to know the facts; they were there when it happened. The competency of the witnesses is further strengthened by their pure moral character. They were good men and women. The charges which were brought against them during their stormy careers were always on some technical, expedient, or ecclesiastical ground, but never once were they convicted of charges or even smeared with rumors of immoral conduct or lack of personal integrity. Strangely enough, chief among all the charges the authorities brought against them was the public "preaching of the resurrection." Stephen died rather than cease to preach it. It was the burden of Peter's sermon at Pentecost and the keynote of Paul's masterful plea before King Agrippa.

Still another effort to discredit the disciples' testimony to the resurrection is based upon the contention that they were gullible and superstitious men. We refute this by appealing to the record again. They at first refused point-blank to believe the women's report, discounting it as rumor and old wives' tales (Luke 24:11). They had finally to be convinced by the presence of the Master, who showed them his nailprints, partook of food in their presence, and rebuked them for their unbelief. Furthermore, the backgrounds from which Jesus had called these men had made them hard and practical, rather than gullible. Sun-tanned fishermen and exacting tax-gatherers are everything but gullible. They are shrewd and bargaining and not easily fooled by anyone. "They had to be shown," and they were. Thomas would not believe until he had seen him with his eyes and felt his death wounds with his hands. While Thomas is singled out as the doubter, there was this eyewitness insistence on the part of the rest of the disciples; and, like Thomas, they would not believe until this insistence had been thoroughly satisfied. We would expect this from impetuous Peter, exacting Matthew, bargaining James and John—the picture we get of them in the preresurrection days. But we would not and could not suspect them of gullibility.

Other objectors to the belief in his bodily resurrection say that the disciples' story of the Easter event was born of delusion. They merely thought they actually saw Christ risen, when as a matter of fact it was a mere mental image, the flash of a trance or a strange vision. We could possibly assent to this if the some six hundred people who are said to have seen him had been constantly under the care of physicians in a psychopathic ward. But even then there would be the difficulty of explaining the strange phenomenon of several hundred people having exactly the same trance or vision about the same person! Such would be an inexhaustible subject of research for the abnormal psychologists, but in all the fantastic gyrations of the human mind nothing like this has ever been encountered. If six hundred depositions and eyewitnesses testified that they had seen a certain person alive, any court of justice in the land would consider such evidence competent and overwhelming. If this were delusion, furthermore, then delusion has meant more to life than truth, and we should have more of it; but we are compelled to say that we cannot discredit as mere illusion that one thing which has meant so much to the life of mankind.

What possible motive could the disciples have had for perpetrating such an illusion or falsehood? In the bitter end it was their testimony to their Lord's resurrection that cost them their precious lives. The first arrest the authorities made among them fell on Peter and John for the public preaching of the resurrection. It was for the public preaching of the resurrection that Paul was incarcerated in two prisons and hailed before Felix, King Agrippa, and the emperor at Rome (Acts 26:22–23). It was for this same cause that he was finally beheaded. Men do not die for illusions, lies, or idle tales. They of the disciples' caliber die only for truth. They could have recanted and gone on living. They chose suffering and death instead; and a fact about which there was the slightest doubt in their minds would not have inspired such heroism. Death from evil hands became so common among these witnesses of the resurrection that the words "witness" and "martyr" became synonymous. And the "witness" was always linked with the resurrection.

The reliability of the disciples' testimony is further undergirded by the test of ordinary logic. There are only three possibilities concerning the question of his resurrection: First, he lay in the grave and decomposed. Secondly, he was stolen away. Thirdly, he arose from the dead. If he lay in the grave and decomposed, why did his enemies not produce his corpse and thus brand the apostles as liars and scatter their followers? This was not done. If he were stolen away, by whom? By his foes? Then why did they not exhibit his body at the opportune time and make fools of those who were preaching his resurrection? This they never did.

Was he stolen away by his friends? How could they have accomplished so daring a feat, except by force or bribery? For the former they were too impotent, what with a sentry of Roman soldiers guarding the tomb. For the latter they were too poor. The only other possibility is that he arose from the dead.

Our final consideration of the reality of this Easter event is based upon the historical effects of the resurrection. The sophists who would explain away the body of evidence presented above will find this more difficult, if not impossible, to gainsay or dislodge. When we move among these postludes of Easter morning we discover five new creations that can be tracked back to an open tomb and a risen Lord. First of all, the resurrection created a new day—the Lord's Day. Every week in which the Lord's Day rolls around is a present proof of the resurrection, as there was only the Jewish Sabbath before the first Easter morning. Most ancient and revered of all the Jewish institutions, this Sabbath was soon supplanted by the following day, the "Lord's Day," the first day of the week, in the worship of the Christians of the early centuries (Acts 20:7; Rev. 1:10), and expressly so because on that day their Master arose from the dead. Every Sunday is, in reality, Easter Sunday, because it is in celebration of Jesus' rising from the dead.

Thus the Lord's Day is a weighty argument for the historical resurrection; that is, for a resurrection which has a place and weight among datable events.

In the second place, the resurrection created a new Church. It came into being at Pentecost, fifty days after Easter, through the power and operation of the Holy Spirit. This power and infilling of the Spirit, through which came the revelation of universal salvation and the birth of the Church of Christ, was the enlarging continuation of the Power that robbed death of its victory in Joseph's tomb. It was that which was promised by Christ after he had risen when he declared: "All authority in heaven and on earth has been given to me . . . thus it behoved me to suffer, and to rise from the dead the third day . . . and ye are witnesses of these things . . . behold, I send the promise of my Father upon you . . . tarry ye in Jerusalem, until ye be endued with power from on high." This power came at Pentecost, and the Church was born. If Peter's memorable sermon had stopped at Calvary, there would have been no Pentecost. But it went on to include the resurrection, and the Church was born and spread its power over the world. In Nero's day, Tacitus tells us that "Christians were a vast multitude." Tertullian of the second century said: "We are but of yesterday and have filled all places among you." Irenaeus added to the shout with the observation that "Christians are scattered over all the earth."

In the third place, the resurrection event created a new people. They were so strange that they were called a "third race." They were first called "Christians" at Antioch. We see the first evidences of this new people in a changed apostolic life. Something happened to the disciples between Calvary and Pentecost that made bold martyrs from the plastic clay of weaklings and cowards. It was the dynamite of their Lord's resurrection. Peter, who denied him, and would again go afishing, dealt the master stroke at Pentecost that gave birth to the Church, and ere deny him again trod the Via Dolorosa alone and suffered death on a cross with his head downward. James and John who were once selfish, conceited office seekers, and who argued with Christ to burn the cities that would not receive them, were turned into daring servants of righteousness and love, the one suffering the headsman's block, the other exile far away. All because they had seen the risen Lord and made bold to proclaim it everywhere they went. "We cannot but speak the things which we have seen and heard," they exclaimed. Except as risen and exalted, they never preached Jesus at all. It was this indwelling of the resurrection spirit that had changed their lives. And through the same spirit they changed others; so much so, in fact, that the early Christians were executed under the same death penalty as magicians, because they, like the magicians, were guilty of changing lives!

In the fourth place, the resurrection created a new book—the New Testament. The resurrection was being preached, propagated, and was bearing its fruit in the early Church before the Gospels or any other part of the New Testament were written. The New Testament, therefore, certainly did not create the resurrection. The resurrection created the New Testament. It is doubtful whether a single line of it would have been written, had Jesus not projected his life and power beyond Calvary into the contemporary life of its authors. They simply had to tell that story because of its fine triumphant ending—or does it have an ending? The gospel, "good news," which it proclaims is inseparably bound up with the good news of the resurrection.

In the fifth place, the resurrection created a new hope. It was an ever living hope of eternal life and immortality. As an old man, Simon Peter was still jubilant with this new hope, basing it always on Christ's resurrection. He exclaimed: "We have been born anew to a living hope through the resurrection of Jesus Christ from the dead, and to an inheritance which is imperishable, undefiled, and unfading, kept in heaven for you, who by God's power are guarded through faith for a salvation ready to be revealed in the last time." (I Peter 1:3–5) And so with the rest of the disciples and Paul, who longed to know "the power of his resurrection, and the fellowship of his sufferings . . . if by any means I might attain unto the resurrection of the dead." This new hope expressed itself in a daily risen life and it was based upon the "first fruits of them that slept." In the Epilogue we shall examine this hope more fully.

Easter as It Relates
to Life Today

*

The resurrection remains today a high commentary upon the genuineness of Jesus. "Jesus is risen. Jesus is Lord. Jesus is Christ. Jesus is genuine." These were all synonymous thoughts and terms with the disciples, the last declaration always following and depending upon the first. The fact that he came from over an old-fashioned hill called Calvary, where he died for the truth he proclaimed, and the further fact that when crushed to earth he arose again, crowns with eternal significance every word he uttered, every promise he made, and every magnanimous deed he performed. This Easter event settled the question of his being the Messiah sent from God to redeem the world. In the opening line of Romans, Christ is declared or constituted "the Son of God in power by the resurrection from the dead." It stamped him as genuine.

Upon this genuineness of Jesus, made complete by his victory over death, the living hope of life eternal and immortality has its sure foundation. It was so with the first disciples and it is so with us. Whatever may have happened in the grave and in the appearances, one thing is certain: from this grave the indestructible faith in the conquest of death and in an eternal life has taken its origin. The resurrection, therefore, is more than a fact. It is a gospel which has brought "immortality to light," and those first disciples kept that light beating against all the darkness of the world. Imbued with the quickening power of this new hope, they moved across the face of their century and changed its whole complexion.

St. Paul declared: "If in this life only we have hope in Christ, we are of all men most miserable." James Denney, in his *Jesus and the Gospel*, points out with significance that "life is determined by the kind of motives which enter into it. If a man believes, as Paul did, in the risen Christ and in the immortal life beyond death, motives from that sphere of reality will enter into his life here, and give it a new character; and it will be time enough to disparage the morality of this verse when we find the people who dispense with the apostolic motive leading the apostolic life. That man would be of all men most miserable who ran a race for a hope set before him, and found when he had reached the goal that he himself and the hope and all that had inspired him crumbled into dust. It is in the same temper that the apostle writes immediately afterwards: 'If after the manner of men I have fought with beasts at Ephesus, what doth it profit me? If the dead are not raised, let us eat and drink, for tomorrow we die.' This is not a childish petulance, as if he had said, 'I will not be good unless I get to heaven.' It is rather the passionate expression of the feeling that if goodness and all that is identified with it is not finally victorious—in a word, is not eternal—there is no such thing as goodness at all. If life is bounded by time, men will live in one way; if it has an outlook beyond death, they will live in another way, for the range and balance of their motives will be different." In other words, this new hope adds to our little text of time the great context of eternity. The self-styled enlightened man who insists that virtue is its own reward and that we ought all to live up to the very highest regardless of the life beyond, might well consider this point.

In the second place, the resurrection demonstrates that our religion is at once subjective and objective. It means that our religion has moved from the subjective to the objective realm—that there is something at both ends. When prayer for many has been reduced to an exercise in auto-suggestion or mental gymnastics, the resurrection is especially significant for us today. E. Stanley Jones reminds us that, "to be Christ, Jesus simply had to rise from the dead in order to round out a ministry to all the needs and desires of life—the spiritual, the mental, and the physical. In the resurrection the circle was completed," and tangibility was given to the life and operations of the unseen. God does break through the scenes to crush evil and uphold and reward righteousness. He does answer prayer. Reality is nearer the end of faith than we know, and a waiting, listening, and answering God is at the end of prayer. As water is the answer to thirst, light the answer to the eye, and food the answer to hunger, eternal life, now real and overwhelming, is the answer to the soul's invincible surmise.

Evil raises the cross on a high hill, exclaiming to all: "See, I triumph today." The might of God thunders back out of an open tomb, replying: "But wait. There is always tomorrow. See my Son and our Cause more glorious and alive than ever. I go marching on. I prevail!"

Once the world has been convinced of this, there comes in the face of doubt and confusion a deep abiding certitude as to the innate worth of life. Even the best of lives are moody with gnawing melancholia and clouded with hours of futility. The roads of life are high and hard, and many a lone pilgrim pauses in the steep climb to wonder if the summit is worth the crosses which must be borne on the upward way. Now since the Easter dawning there is one who proved his strength with this treacherous Everest, and he meets us in the way to tell us that we are higher than the highest hill, and this present suffering and struggling is "not worthy to be compared with the glory which shall be revealed in us."

Is the good life worth while? Is it more than meat, and drink, and raiment? Are the high goals which challenge us from afar worth the pierced hands and the broken hearts which at the last must beat out their pain upon some Calvary? As we grope in this sort of questioning, we come out face to face with the glory of a risen Lord, who, by the fact of his resurrection, assures us that Calvary is not the last chapter in the lives of us who dare to follow him. We have always known that our destiny is tied up with him, and his resurrection gives us reason to believe that this destiny shall be meaningful and kind. "If it were not so, I would have told you," declared Jesus.

In the third place, the resurrection gives spiritual content to the *quality* of our daily living. It not only sheds light on the question of the duration of our life, but also on the question of *kind*. The quantity of our days is one thing, and the quality of our days is another. We are not only interested in the question, How long is our life?, but we are also interested in the question, What is it like? The resurrection experience in the life of Jesus exalted and glorified him, and as a result of its inspiration and power, the disciples began to experience *eternal living* immediately. They had always believed in an immortality, of a sort. They had now come to believe joyously in eternal life. Thus, Christ reestablishes our faith in the kind of life to which he has called us.

Vested with the light and power of a risen Christ, life awakens to its divine capacities and its deep significance and feels that it deserves to go on forever. One would hardly desire to continue forever a narrowing routine of pettiness and meanness. Perhaps the strongest argument for immortality is one person I know who deserves an endless life. You see, men first lose faith in this life before they dismiss the next as a poet's dream. But the Lord of Life lifts us from our bestial natures and opens our eyes to see our inexhaustible possibilities, and on this ground we dare to believe that life is stronger than death—that our lives shall continue forever.

In a deeper wisdom than we know, Simon Peter exclaimed at Pentecost: "It was not possible that Christ should be holden of death." According to him, it would have been a greater miracle if Jesus had *not* risen from the dead! The resurrection quality of living, therefore, leads us to believe that no tomb on earth, however strongly guarded, can imprison forever those of us who have carried the image of the Lord Jesus in our hearts through the years. It moves us to join with George Matheson who said: "Son of Man, whenever I despair of life I think on Thee. Nothing is so impossible as that Thou shouldst be dead."

Finally, the resurrection furnishes us the only basis for a genuine optimism. In our low moments, we view life's highest and most beautiful experiences and utter under our breath, "That would be wonderful if it were true, but it is too good to be true." Too good to be true, but it is true! This is the gospel of the resurrection. It is too good to be true that Mary Magdalene should quit the unchaste streets of Magdala and set her feet on the chastity of the King's highway. But it is true. It is too good to be true that drunkards quit their drink and thieves their stealing, but it is true. It is too good to be true that sinners like you and me have been saved from their ignoble purposes, their animal appetites, and the disillusionment that comes from pagan conduct. But it is true. After all, the resurrection eloquently tells us that we live in a world where Job gets well more often than he dies, where Rachel will cease to mourn for her brood, and where Jesus Christ rises from the dead!

Here at last is the mighty Conqueror of the forces that are every day destroying our lives. To every Christian of us who is trying desperately hard to outwill and outwit the sinister plagues of character, he rings his invincible spirit in our souls: "In the world ye shall have tribulation: but be of good cheer; I have overcome the world." When we feel the life back of such a voice, we know that all human life has dignity and worth and is sound and sweet at bottom. Under him we are convinced that we are bigger than anything that can happen to us. Like him, bigger than sorrow, bigger than disease, bigger than disappointment, bigger than sin, bigger than heartbreak, and bigger than death. Even so, our Lord gives us a haunting picture of what our humanity can become when it takes on the whole mantle of divinity. By virtue of the conquering love and power he has bestowed upon us, we can become strong eternal fellows, even the sons and daughters of God. This is the work of the miracle—resurrection! There is enough beauty and wonder in this one thought to grip and hold us our whole life through.

Friedrich Rittelmeyer, in his *Behold the Man,* sums up the life and resurrection of Jesus with meaning and power as few have done: "The coming of a Conqueror into the world with a symphony of qualities and powers which render him sure that all fearsome things, human and super-human, have forever lost their fearsomeness, and the overcoming by this Conqueror of all that is hardest and all that is darkest through the power of his unquenchable consciousness of victory—that is the story of Jesus."

This is his story. It is also our story. We in whom the resurrection has already begun will repeat this story over and over again as the good news to our own souls and to a world living in quiet desperation. This deathless story is strength to the man whose sins are tearing his life to pieces. It is hope to the unfinished life whose plans require an eternity for fulfillment. It is a sweet courage to those who have fainted and fallen in the way. It is a comfort to those whose loved ones left them in the long ago and took their hearts with them when they went away. With us always in this life, Christ will not desert us in the next. As Joseph Fort Newton once declared: "He who filled our hearts with the haunting hopes of an eternal tomorrow will not leave us in the dust."

When ten thousand springs have come and sung their green way into summer's golden heart, this story of our mighty Conqueror will still be fresh and new to lend its glad power over life and death to all who seek a bolstering against their faltering mortality. Even then the resurrection will still be declaring: "All things, including eternal life, belong to you who belong to God!"

Epilogue

THIS NEW HOPE

This New Hope

*

From the Christian point of view, hope is the expectation of good. It is toiling through the long days with a look toward some enchanted evening. It is Shelley singing in the night, "If winter comes, can spring be far behind?" Hope is a pilgrimage, punctuated at the end by a light in the window of home. It is captive Daniel in a foreign land, climbing the steps to his chamber thrice daily, and opening his balcony door toward the Holy City.

Hope has always traveled in great company, with faith on the left and love on the right. It is thus one of the three everlastings, as indicated by the apostle Paul. "And now abideth faith, hope and charity." The writer to the Hebrews could not define faith without hope, nor can love be experienced or fulfilled without it. All faith is empty, and all love is meaningless, save where there is hope. When hope has vanished, all has vanished, and nothing is possible. When hope is alive, all things are alive, and anything is possible.

Life has three dimensions: memory, experience, and hope. When the third is alive, the other two are full of sweet song and salt and grace. When hope has died, then memory and experience stand still, looking sad.

These are the words St. Luke used in the twenty-fourth chapter of his Gospel, to describe the two disciples on the Emmaus road, the third day after the crucifixion. "They stood still, looking sad." They were walking the somber road of despair, wounded and sick from "a dream grown thin." They thought the light in the Lord of Life had been put out forever. With that light guttered, their hopes had crumbled. As they stumbled along their lonesome way, they mumbled under their breath, "We had hoped . . . we had hoped that he was the one to redeem Israel."

This inscribed picture of hopelessness is most expressive of the mood of our times. No generation ever hoped for so much as ours and realized so little from its hopes. So that the despairing cry of Cleopas and his companion has become our cry, "We had hoped . . . we had hoped . . ." It is the cry of the world, and the grief of the Church: "We had hoped . . ." In some of our churches and most of our world one would think that the hopeful Christian drama fell into shambles at Calvary— that the gospel ended with the crucifixion.

The reasons for such despair are so evident that it is painful to point them out. Some of the world's hopes have been foolish and others diabolical. Our Christian hopes have, on the whole, been legitimate and good but, generally speaking, they have not been nurtured by the long look, the large picture, and the loving heart, irreducible minimums for the fruition of any great hope. Most specifically, we may have hoped *for* the right consummations, but we have hoped *in* the wrong means for their realization.

We have hoped *for* the perfect man, but we have hoped *in* a perfect set of external circumstances to produce him. That a perfect man will follow from a perfect set of circumstances, is the gigantic delusion of all time. Adam and Eve found that out a long time ago! We have hoped *for* the abundant life, but we have hoped *in* science to bring it about. With science as our shepherd, we still want. For we see now that when science opens one door, it usually closes another. Science opened the door on externalism and closed the door on the life of the spirit. It opened the door on immediacy and closed the door on the long look. It opened the door on noise and closed the door on creative solitude. It opened the door on mass production and closed the door on the personal touch. It opened the door on speed and closed the door on the delights of the journey. If Gabriel should land from heaven on our city streets this morning, I suppose the first question we would ask him would be, "Gabriel, how long did it take you to make it?"

We have hoped *for* world peace, but we have hoped *in* pacts, treaties, spheres of influence, and in fine balances of power to usher in this clean, white blessing.

We have hoped *for* a united Church, but we have hoped *in* a regimentation of doctrine and life that was as unknown to the early Christians as Goethe's *Faust* and as foreign to the spirit of Jesus as Satan himself. We have hoped *for* the evangelization of the world, but we have hoped *in* denominational segments instead of a global Christian offensive. We have hoped *for* that "one far-off, divine event," but we have hoped *in* the inevitability of progress, taking too literally the remainder of the poet's words, "to which the whole creation moves." We now see that pendulums do not swing. They are pushed. And progress is far from inevitable.

To put it in other words, our ends for the most part have been excellent, but our means have been inferior. We have had our destination pretty clearly in mind, but we have caught the wrong bus. So we are tired of the journey. Too much frustration. Too many disillusionments. Too much strife. Too far to travel yet. Too long to wait. And like the Emmaus disciples we sigh: "We had hoped . . . we had hoped . . ." Or like one of our contemporaries we say—

I am battered and broken and weary and out of heart,
I will not hear talk of heroic things,
But be content to play some simple part . . .
Men were not meant to walk as priests and kings.

It was to this kind of psychology and this sort of gloom that the apostles Paul and Peter spoke in the first century. St. Paul declared: "We have not been disgraced by our hopes, because God's love has been poured into our hearts." St. Peter added: "We have been born anew to a living hope through the resurrection of Jesus Christ from the dead . . . to an inheritance which is imperishable, undefiled, and unfading, kept in heaven for you, who by God's power are guarded through faith."

Here the two great apostles laid down the two sure sources and inextricably bound them together, for secure and genuine hope: the love of God in our wistful and anxious hearts, and the resurrection of Christ as an event affecting our personal destiny in and beyond time. These sure sources not only anchor us in our legitimate hopes; they also hold forth to us the noble means for their attainment. In a word, our hopes will be Christian, and they will never disgrace us, as long as we are conscious subjects of God's redeeming love; and the attainment of our Christian hopes is guaranteed either in time or in eternity by the resurrection of Jesus Christ from the dead.

Our interior lives will be renewed again when we lay fresh hold upon the love of God, for this is our first hope. Think on God's love! How unutterably extravagant. It is tender like a shepherd's, tenacious like a cross, and triumphant like the living presence beyond an open tomb. This love is a "supporting tendency" toward a better world, and apart from such a tendency we struggle forward without a sense of direction and without any reasonable hope.

Edwin E. Aubrey put it this way: "To say that God is love is to say that deep in the cosmic order is a movement toward unity of spirit, sensitive mutual understanding, acute concern for our fellows, readiness to give ourselves up that another may profit. Nowhere is this more powerfully manifest than in the life and death of Jesus Christ our Lord. It is this love of God, shown in Jesus Christ and flooding our lives, that vindicates our struggles and validates our hope. That love does not fail us in the end. In its light we have shaped our best thoughts and aspirations, borne our bitterest grief, endured our most heartbreaking disappointments, lifted up our heads to learn from our tribulations, and built up our expectations of greater good to come."

This sense of God's love is basic to our staying power and basic to our hope. Let God's love flood our lives again, and we shall have a hope as old as God and as new as this morning's sunrise. And we shall discover that, if faith makes all things possible, God's love makes all things easy.

Several years ago a church in London was torn by strife to the point of closing its feeble ministry and padlocking the door. First God's love died. Then hope vanished from the hearts of most of the members. A mass meeting of the membership was held for the final, corporate rites. Seated near the front of the sanctuary was the half-wit of the church. Listening intently to the strident voices of tension and despair, the half-wit arose and walked to the chancel. He faced the crowd, then lifted his eyes toward the ceiling and began: "You love me, God, and I love you." Then he started stumbling through the English alphabet, every letter of it, from A through Z. "Dear God, take our love for each other and these letters and make up the words that are in my heart and put them into theirs." The deathlike silence that had gripped the crowd was quickly broken by intermittent sobbing. Then, like a sweep of wings, the audience arose as one man and sang the Doxology through their tears. Needless to say, that church never closed. It found new hope in the simple love of God that burned in the heart of a half-wit.

> *O wondrous is his love for all*
> *Who seek it, though in bleak despair,*
> *And find it moving through the pall,*
> *Because his face is shining there.*

Now let us look more deeply into the second source of this new hope, as experienced by Simon Peter in the resurrection of Jesus from the dead. He was saying that, in spite of Calvary, Jesus of Nazareth in his resurrection had renewed his person and his message in the life of his contemporaries. Something glorious and tremendous had happened. Something that moved the first Christian community to exclaim, "We have been born anew to a life of hope by the renewal of his life in ours." Jesus of Nazareth had become Jesus the Christ.

This power of Jesus Christ to renew his spirit in human life from generation to generation is at once an abiding source of perennial hope and the marvel of the ages. How often does he still appear among us on the dusty road, "closer than breathing and nearer than hands and feet." How often does he still walk the lonely ways of our deserted altars to inhabit their dead shrines with new life and hope and bringing us back to our lost saints and to the simple faith and the first loves of our childhood. And how recently has he been invading with new charm and power our dry baptistries, our empty pews, and our powerless pulpits. O Son of Man, O Son of God, this day Thou hast renewed Thy life even in me! This realistic experience is most assuredly an inexhaustible source of deathless hope for us all.

A Nazi guard surprised a home prayer meeting in a section of Hitler's Germany, which our troops later overran. As I got the story, they had violated the law by having more than five people together without special permission. Inquiring as to how many were present, the guard was told by the prayer leader that there were thirteen. But the guard could count only twelve. He proceeded to discipline the leader for lying, whereupon the leader pointed to a vacant chair and explained: "You see, sir, there are really thirteen present. Our Lord, who promised to be with us, is sitting in that vacant chair." They would not have believed that of Bismarck, nor of Kaiser Wilhelm, nor of Hitler. But they believed it of their Lord and found it true. Our Master says, "I am with you always," and lo, we think upon him and find it true. To our sick and penitent souls he says, "Your sins are forgiven," and we rise, take up our beds and walk away, cleansed and full of peace. He commands us to go and make disciples of all the nations, and we find ourselves going without a single question. He promises, "Come unto me, all ye that labour and are heavy laden, and I will give you rest." We come, and "around our incompleteness flows his greatness and round our restlessness his rest." We would not believe that of any other dead or living soul, but we know it to be true of him.

So I repeat that the power of Jesus to renew his spirit in human life in every generation is not only a source of our perennial hope but it is also the marvel of the ages.

If you do not believe this, ponder the fact that, once Jesus has renewed himself in us, we immediately begin to see new vistas opening for us beyond the bounds of this life. We are seized with the confidence that he who gave himself to us when we were born spiritually will not take himself back when we die physically. We believe with St. Paul that "Christ in us is the hope of glory," and that "if in this life only we have hope in Christ, we are of all men most miserable." We rejoice with the great apostle that eye has not seen, ear has not heard, nor has it entered into the heart of man, the things that God has prepared for them that love him. We hold that all Christian hopelessness is premature.

The Emmaus disciples found it so when the night

was gathering. The unknown risen one to whom they unburdened their hopelessness became their new hope as he appeared between them and caused their hearts to burn within them as he talked with them along the way. And what they discovered then, we steadfastly believe today: Every genuine disciple of Christ, in one way or another, has a great future. With Simon Peter we become stockholders in that great "inheritance kept for us in heaven, imperishable, undefiled, and unfading." We are captured with the faith that we will live forever in the economy of a loving Father, because of our risen Lord who said: "Because I live, you shall live also."

During the Second World War the infantry division of which I was the senior Protestant chaplain cornered in a large forest an S.S. German division, the cruelest of Hitler's lot. Our Intelligence had found that they were in dire straits. Their lines of communication had been cut, their lines of supply broken. So they had run out of food and their ammunition was reaching the vanishing point. They could not contact their headquarters. Our commanding general ordered them to surrender or die. They died. But with us it was different. Our lines of communication and supply were intact. Food, ammunition, and medical supplies were coming through, and we were in constant touch with our headquarters. We lived. The chief difference between the enemy and us lay in the fact that they were cut off from too much to live and we were linked up with too much to die!

This analogy holds true between Christians with the Easter hope and those without it. The love of God and the indwelling spirit of Jesus have linked us up with too much to die. Without the conscious experience of either, millions are cut off from too much to live. As someone has said: "They are like children in a kindergarten, trying to spell life with the wrong blocks." Vachel Lindsay lamented: "Not that they starve, but they starve so dreamlessly. Not that they die, but that they die like sheep."

Immanuel Kant said there are only three fundamental questions in human life: "What can I know? For what can I hope? And, in view of these two, what must I do?" We of the Beloved Community know the love of God. We hope in the life of Jesus, eternal in character and duration, renewing himself in ours. And it is for us, with this living hope, to attune the ears of the world's people to hear "the far-sent message of the years" and turn their eyes to see "the glory of the coming Light."